/2○

YE SHALL BE COMFORTED

THE WESTMINSTER PASTORAL AID BOOKS
Russell L. Dicks, General Editor

YE SHALL BE COMFORTED

by William F. Rogers, Ph.D.

Philadelphia
THE WESTMINSTER PRESS

Grateful acknowledgment is expressed to:

Advance, for permission to use "What Is Steel?" by Stanley E. Anderson.

Harper & Brothers, for the use of the following selections from the *Book of Comfort,* compiled by Eric Parker, 1945: "They Live" and "How to Bear Sorrow," by Charles Kingsley; "Robin Elliott," by Canon W. H. Elliott; and "Comrades Still," by Bishop John Maud.

Houghton Mifflin Company, for the use of the selections from Whittier and Tennyson.

The Macmillan Company, for permission to use "Prayer with a Bereaved Person," from *Comfort Ye My People,* by Russell L. Dicks, 1947; and also for the use of the following selections from *The Faith of Man Speaks,* edited by H. Woodbury, 1945: "Prayer in Bereavement," from *The Union Prayer-Book for Jewish Worship;* "A Prayer," by Samuel Johnson; "Immortal Child," by Saint John Chrysostom; "Consolation," by Elizabeth Barrett Browning; selection from Homer's *Iliad;* "Keep Me from Bitterness," Anonymous; selections from John Donne and Cicero; "The Summons," by John Bunyan; "The New Edition," by Benjamin Franklin.

To
RUTH

without whose encouragement and considerable help this work would never have
been undertaken, much less completed

As one whom his mother comforteth,
So will I comfort you;
And ye shall be comforted in Jerusalem.
                              —Isaiah 66:13

CONTENTS

FOREWORD

THE POSSIBLE LOSS of a loved one through death is one of the haunting dreads that lurks in the mind of most persons. Whenever grief comes, we are unprepared for it. This fact is increasingly true, for death has been described as "a taboo subject in this generation." We do not like to think about it and we prefer not to talk about it. We hide the reality of death away in a dark closet of our minds and try to forget it. There is no indication that the trend will change in the immediate future; in fact, we expect this ostrichlike way of handling one of life's major crises to increase.

But death *is* real. It *does* exist, both for ourselves and for our loved ones. To be sure it is pushed farther and farther away through the discoveries of medical science, but it still comes sooner or later to everyone.

It is the purpose of this book to deal helpfully and realistically with the age-old problem of grief. The first part of the book is based upon medical and psychiatric research of recent years, and the second part contains selected observations and proclamations of the faith of the ages. It contains the new and the old, and bridges the gap between the two.

The third chapter, which deals with *who can help and how* when grief comes, is probably the most significant single chapter in any book dealing with the problems of living that has been written in this century. It contains material the truth of which we have long suspected, simply and understandably presented. People have known for a long time that they were helped through severe experiences of emotional suffering by talking with someone in whom they had confidence and who supported them through love and affection. Here Dr. Rogers describes the process of seeking help, who can give it and how; he tells us also how to choose one who can help us, and describes signs that should warn one away from a person who cannot help. The great danger which we all recognize here is the emotional dependency that one who is suffering from grief may come to feel toward the one who seeks to help him. Hence the importance of seeking help from one who is a disciplined and skilled person in this type of ministry. In every church, in every community, there are such persons, who, with a little encouragement and the opportunity, can be of great help to their neighbors and friends when the heavy darkness of grief closes down upon them.

I would recommend that this book be read before grief comes, by way of preparation for it, and again after grief has arrived. If a given chapter, passage of Scripture, or poem, particularly appeals to you, mark it, so that you may come back to it readily.

Grief is a destructive force, violent in its attack, grim in its persistency; unless one is liberated from it in a reasonably short time after it comes, that is, within six weeks to three months, it may become as vicious a destroyer of the human spirit as cancer is of the physical body. This is a book that will help to stop the destructive force of grief.

RUSSELL L. DICKS.

PART ONE

WHEN GRIEF COMES

WHEN LOVED ONES DIE

THE DEATH of a loved one is a painful experience, not because we fear what has happened or is happening to the loved one, but because of the loneliness that we ourselves are suffering. Our loved one is gone and there is only an aching void where once he was. The emptiness and change that have come to our lives are a bitter portion indeed. The experience is the more distressing because the ache is deep where no palliative can reach it. The cure lies in the healing processes of the spirit, which we can aid if we understand.

Grief comes from separation. Usually we think of it in relationship to loss from death. This is the most common and drastic form of separation, but other separations are painful too. The young boy who goes to camp and becomes very homesick is grieving over his separation from familiar companionships. The deserted husband or wife is likely to grieve as if the partner had died. War separations brought many instances of acute grief. Death, however, produces the most acute and recognized cases of grief. Let us think about it in this setting.

We are social beings. We live in close interaction with our fellow men. This is especially true of our parents, husband or wife, or children. The whole pattern of our own lives includes actions and thoughts that have meaning only because the partner is there to share them with us. From our parents we get not only physical food, but emotional support as well. If our parents love us and show their affection, we feel confident and trustful toward life. If they express appreciation for us and our accomplishments, we have the recognition that all men need. This need to feel secure and to be recognized stays with us all through our lives. As adults, we get support from husbands or wives, or from the love of our children, or from some other individual who becomes close to us in our daily lives. Loved ones become a real part of our own lives and personalities; in marriage, for example, in a real sense, the two become one.

The breaking of this close relationship results in grief. Death brings a virtual loss of one's larger self as the whole range of activities that were tied up in the deceased disappear. This is often acutely illustrated where the bereaved has long taken care of the deceased, as the woman who for years cared for her mother. Death of the mother may bring relief, but it also brings an end to the need for care and the whole pattern of life which the daughter has built up around this need. Perhaps a better illustration is a woman who has lost her husband, and the whole pattern of her housekeeping, which had been built around his likes and needs, no longer has meaning. There is an empty place at the table, and the foods that once were prepared for his special satisfaction now seem to have lost their reason for being prepared. Meal schedules no longer have to be fitted into his work schedule. Instead of " his " and " hers " towels hanging in the bathroom, there is only " hers." The whole foundation of her habit pattern is gone, and meaninglessness as well as loneliness sets in. The more intimate the relationship and the more completely the life of the bereaved has been tied up with the deceased, the more acute the resulting grief will be.

With death our loved one is gone. But memories linger on. At the center of them, usually, is a mental picture of the deceased. Often it is a distressing picture. We see our loved one ready for the last trip to the hospital, or with his features wasted from a long illness. Some particular situation keeps coming back before our mind's eye over and over again, and we have to cope with all the memories that cluster around this picture. Often these memories will be painful as they renew the pain we felt when we saw the loved one suffer. Always they are painful because of the realization that the one whom we now remember is no longer with us. This pain is an integral and necessary part of grief.

The pain of grief is expressed most acutely in periods of sobbing in which the whole body is shaken by distress. When some especially vivid memory comes, or when one thinks or talks of the deceased, these periods are sure to come. They come when the time arrives for carrying out some plans that the deceased and the bereaved had made together, as, for example, the taking of a particular trip which a married couple had been planning for some time, but which the wife never lived to carry out. The hour of departure was particularly painful for the widower as he remembered the hours of anticipation he and his wife had had together. These periods come when a photograph or a memento of some kind brings back thoughts of pleasant times together. They come when friends call to sympathize and to talk about the deceased. These times, many of them, come when grief is directly, honestly, and courageously faced.

Between periods of sobbing, one can expect to feel a more general discomfort. There is a restlessness which makes it difficult to sit still or to relax. One feels the need to be doing something all the time. At the same time, however, it is difficult to undertake any task and stick to it. The restlessness brings difficulty in finding satisfaction with any activity for any sustained length of time. Even tasks that had become habitual seem to lose not only their meaning, but their habit pattern. One has to face, during the period of acute grief, the distress of the need to be active and the inability of being able to concentrate on any particular activity.

To understand grief best, think of it as an emotion. Certain things that we know about emotions will help us to understand better this thing that happens to us when loved ones die.

The first factor to consider is that in emotion there is a disturbance of the glandular functioning of the body. In slight positive emotions, such as joy, there is a stimulation of the normal glandular functioning of the body, but in strong negative emotions, such as sadness, there is, for example, a cessation of the flow of digestive fluids. This accounts in part at least for the physical distress mentioned above. It also indicates the need for a proper meeting of one's grief problem. An undue delay in doing the necessary mourning can cause physical difficulties of serious consequence.

Another factor in emotion is that it is a conscious condition. That is to say, it can be forced out of consciousness, and thus be denied or delayed. In grief there is the conscious pain of loneliness which can be escaped by refusing to admit one's loss, or by refusing to think about the deceased. One can consciously avoid the physical distress and the pain of loneliness that come with grief by the simple process of refusing to think about the deceased. This is often done by disposing of all the belongings of the deceased, and everything that would remind one of him. A man who has lost his wife may escape the pain of grief by selling all the furniture, and even the house, that the two had used together, and moving to a new neighborhood. He may give away all her clothes, and discard all pictures and mementos. By entering into a new mode of life he is successful, at least for a time, in forgetting his wife, and thus avoiding the pain of grief.

Instead of pushing out all memory, one may deny the loss, and say, perhaps unconsciously, " It isn't so — my loved one hasn't died." This illusion may be kept alive in various ways. A man may quickly remarry. In so doing he may identify his second wife with his first. " See," he may say in effect, " my wife didn't die — here she is — just like always." Experience may gradually teach him that this is not the same woman, but the illusion may be kept alive for some time. The denial may take the form of an imaginary companionship with the deceased. An empty chair at the deceased's place at the table may be the prelude to a running conversation, with imaginary answers serving as reality. A daily report as by letter may carry the news of one's activities to the " temporarily " absent loved one. Where the two have been working together in some endeavor, " consultation " may go on in planning the next steps of the work, and mutual evaluation may help to appraise the work done.

Since emotion is a conscious state, it may be denied or delayed by various methods of pushing it out of consciousness. Periods of sobbing may be avoided, and feelings of loneliness may be escaped, either through conscious suppression or through unconscious repression of the memories that bring them on. However, another attribute of emotion comes into play when this is done. An emotion that is denied expression is not thereby destroyed. It is merely pushed down into the unconscious, where it remains like the confined steam in a pressure cooker. That is, it remains there for a time, until the pressure becomes too strong; then it comes out in some disguised form. The expression may be a case of " nerves " or some physical symptom. " Keeping your chin up " doesn't solve anything. It only fools one into a false pride of maturity that one does not actually possess. Instead of giving a strong expression of faith, one is obtaining a false sense of peace through short-cutting the emotional process. One devil may be chased out only to make room for seven more devilish than the first.

Emotion requires action. Love requires the expression of affection; anger requires attack; and fear requires flight. When in fear, for example, one escapes from the path of the speeding automobile, then the emotion subsides. When an employee, however, fears the loss of his job and the consequent insecurity, and is unable to do anything about it, then the emotion continues, with the consequent continuation of the distress. Grief is an acute, and a difficult, emotion to deal with because of the inability to do anything about the loss which has brought it on.

Another characteristic of emotion that has relevance for us in the study of grief is that when a suppressed emotion is released, other emotions associated with it are likely to be released also. When we grieve for a loved one, we are likely also to feel the anger that we had for him. Not realizing this may cause one to be very much disturbed over the hostile feelings toward the deceased that often come in time of grief. Understanding this fact will aid one in coping with the contradictory feelings that arise.

These contradictory feelings are a powerful and often very disturbing factor in grief. The ability to love someone, and at the same time to feel angry with him, or to have feelings of hostility toward him, makes for inner confusion and pain. The presence of feelings of relief along with the feeling of loss at the death of one who has been a care and a burden may cause considerable distress. Because this is such a universal experience, which is little understood by most of us, and disturbing to us when it is noticed, we need to analyze it.

An infant finds his mother a source of love. He gets from her the food to satisfy his appetite, and thus he receives pleasure. Likewise he receives from her affection, which gives him not only pleasure but a feeling of security as well. To this pleasure and affection he responds with love.

On the other hand, these pleasures may not always be forthcoming when they are desired. The infant may have to wait for his food, or he may have to postpone for a considerable time the obtaining of affection which he desires. This frustration makes for feelings of anger and hostility. The alternation of satisfaction and affection with frustration and displeasure makes for contradictory feelings of love and hostility being present at the same time, for and against the same person.

Later experiences of life tend to amplify this pattern. A child has to deny his drives and desires to achieve harmony with other persons. His parents, who provide him with shelter and food, security and affection, also discipline him and compel him to conform to socially accepted patterns of behavior. Thus those whom he loves become also objects of hostility. Other persons may enter into the pattern. Other children are loved ones, but they are also rivals for parental affections, playthings, and privileges. One's husband or wife is an object of strong affection, but also a source of many irritations. Marriage brings new responsibilities, new demands, new restrictions to one's activities, and often directly clashing opinions and interests. It is safe to say that in any love relationship there is also present the feeling of hostility that is born of personal frustrations and anger situations.

This contradictory pattern may be complicated by the repression of hostile feelings into the unconscious. A child soon learns that the expression of hostile feelings toward his parents defeats his own desire for affection. Such expression endangers his own security, and promptly brings reprisals. In the adult this repression is likely to result from compunctions of the conscience. One does not ordinarily express hostile feelings toward one's mother or life partner or other intimates. If the training of the conscience has been rigid, one does not even admit to oneself that such feelings of hostility exist. Thus they may be totally repressed and driven from awareness.

These feelings are totally repressed — that is, until some experience such as bereavement releases them. The coming of the emotion of grief may release, also, other emotions that have fixed themselves on the same individual. The death of a parent may bring memories of frustrations and feelings of anger that had been long forgotten, or possibly never even noticed before. The death of an invalid mother to whom a daughter had given years of attention and care, with only feelings of affection and concern being conscious, may find that grief brings with it feelings of resentment at having been tied down so long, and even a realization that unconsciously she had wished for the death of her mother so that she might be free from the burden of her care. The death of a husband may release not only grief, but feelings of anger for his lack of expression of affection, his contrary opinion and practice on some important issue, or his shortcomings as a provider. The loss of a child may bring, not only acute grief, but feelings of anger felt on days when he was cross and exasperating.

Contradictory emotions may be one cause of another factor that is often found in grief, namely, guilt feelings. To be aware of great relief at having the care of an invalid lifted from one may cause strong feelings that one ought not to be glad over the loved one's death. We may feel as if we were very much in the wrong to be angry at our loved one who is now dead. We remember with shame the times when we expressed our anger toward the beloved and feel strongly that we should not have done so. It is even more distressing to feel angry now over incidents that did not rouse any conscious anger at the time of their occurrence. If one has a strong conscience, the guilt feelings arising from the recognition of hostile feelings toward the deceased can be very distressing.

Guilt feelings may arise also out of real or fancied neglect or wrongdoing toward the deceased. And, let it be said, guilt can be just as disturbing whether there is any real basis for it or not. A husband may think back and say: " Why didn't I take my wife to see her folks last summer? She would have enjoyed it so much, but now the chance is gone." This thought may distress him very much. Or the thought may be a regret over not having called the physician soon enough, or over not calling a different one from the one called. If the death of the beloved has been accidental, the guilt feelings can be very strong when the bereaved feels that a different behavior on his part might have avoided the accident. This is illustrated by the guilt feelings of the father whose son was killed by a freak accident while carrying out an apparently simple and harmless parental command. Whatever the source of the guilt feelings, they are very often present, and a real complicating factor in grief.

WE WHO MOURN

ANYTHING AS POWERFUL, and with as far-reaching consequences, as grief needs to be intelligently handled. Neglect or mistakes can be much too costly. Let us consider what we can and ought to do about it.

The first necessity is that we face it. Admit that it is present. Accept it as a reality. The ostrichlike practice of trying to pretend that it doesn't exist not only fails to get rid of it but keeps us from handling it intelligently. It isn't heroism to continue on as if nothing had happened. Something *has* happened, and it is the place of heroism to face the realities of life. The hero doesn't run away from life; he lives it to its fullest. Neither is it the part of wisdom to avoid the pain that follows bereavement. Wisdom calls for the policy that will bring the most satisfactory results in the long run. To try to avoid the pain of grief is to find temporary relief only to suffer a greater pain at some future time. Wisdom reveals that nothing is ever settled until it is settled right. Grief can't be settled until it has been faced.

Church folk are likely to say: "But to give way to an expression of grief is a denial of faith. I believe in immortality. I believe that my loved one still lives. It isn't right for me to grieve." There are two errors in this logic. The first is to confuse physical reality with spiritual reality. As Christians, we believe that our loved one does still live, but that doesn't mean that no change has taken place. Physically he is gone. The former companionship is no more. We can't see him, or touch him, or talk to him in the old way. A change has occurred which leaves a permanent emptiness in the place our beloved once occupied. This physical absence is the basis of our grief. Let us not confuse spiritual reality with physical reality.

The other error inherent in considering grief to be incompatible with faith is the implication that faith means avoiding the issues of life. Faith doesn't mean avoiding the issues of life, nor a denial of the pain of life. It means, rather, the ability to meet life full face. It means the courage and power and patience to pass through the darkest depths and to come through on the other side victorious. After his conversion, Saint Paul had great faith, but it led him into many trials and tribulations rather than to ease and escape. Having faith means having greater resources for meeting grief, but it does not mean avoiding or delaying the pain of acknowledging our loneliness.

Face your grief. In the first hours of bereavement there may be numbness from the shock of loss, or a skeptical disbelief that death has actually occurred. Sooner or later, however, there will come a wave of sobbing. Let it come. It is part of grief and nothing to be ashamed of or to feel guilty about. The pain will soon pass, and physically you will be no worse for the experience. Emotionally you will have dissolved some little part of the tension of grief. Periods of sobbing will continue to occur as you think and talk about the deceased. Let them come. As you pass through them, they will eventually lose their power. If you avoid them, their power will increase. It is better to face some pain at first, which after temporary discomfort will pass away, than to escape the pain for a while only to face more devastating forces later on.

Facing grief implies further the acceptance of the memories of the deceased. The visual image that comes may not be very pleasant, but it needs to be thought about, examined, and talked about. The ability to live with the image is the first step toward getting rid of it. The image, however, will not be the only memory to come. It may be the first, and the most persistent for a time, but the whole panorama of our relationship to the deceased will crowd in upon us as we continue to think of our beloved.

Don't rush back to work after the funeral. That is, don't make getting back to the job a means of absorbing yourself in an activity. It is better if the return to one's job can be postponed for a time. This will allow opportunity for reliving in hallowed memory the whole relationship with the beloved. Friends may be well-intentioned, but they are ill-advised when they urge us to rush back to work to escape from the pain of grief. We don't escape it. We just push it down inside to become an inner tension to cause trouble later on. Bereavement is so important an event, and the need for reliving in memory one's relationship to the deceased is so urgent, that the use of vacation or other leave time on this occasion is amply justified.

Having resolved to accept our memories of the deceased, no matter how painful they may be, the next need is to talk about them. Talking helps to release the emotional tension and to dissolve the pain. Each time we tell about a painful experience the pain is dulled just a little more, until finally it becomes bearable. The memories may continue to come back, but their power to hurt has been dissipated.

First memories, and hence talk, of the deceased will center around the last events of the deceased's life. The last hours of an illness may be reviewed in great detail over and over again. In case of sudden death all the events surrounding the occasion of the heart attack, or accident, may be gone over very carefully. In addition to the description of events, we shall be speculating as to possible causes, as well as filling in gaps in our knowledge as to what did actually take place in these last moments.

As the pain of the memories of the last shocking events wears off, our thoughts will begin to work back to the events that preceded the death. After a long illness, for example, there will likely be a review of the gains and losses, the hopes and fears of the last week; and then thoughts will turn back to the beginning of the illness. If one has personally cared for the deceased in this long illness, there may well be a recounting of the details of that care. Whatever comes to mind is reasonable material for discussion, and serves to meet and to pass through the pain of grief. Later, when the immediate past has been cared for, one will want to review the memories of earlier years. Memories won't come in exact chronological sequence, but, in general, later events will tend to be remembered first. As one talks of these, earlier events will come to mind. Eventually thoughts will go back to earliest relationships. For a husband or wife, the time of meeting the beloved and the first impressions may become real again.

As we talk about the deceased, our remarks will include certain topics relative to him. These will not be isolated, but will be well mingled as we spontaneously speak of the memories that occur to us. Most forceful at first will be probably our sense of loss and sorrow. The bereaved is gone, and his going gives us inward pain. It is of this pain that we shall want to speak. We need to tell of what this loss means to us. The emptiness of our lives that results from bereavement becomes vivid as we think of the one who is gone, and talking helps us to express this emptiness and, to some extent, to overcome it.

A large portion of our talk about the deceased will have to do with appreciation. We can talk long and with much feeling about how fine the beloved was. His courage in the last illness and suffering can be told often, with many illustrations and examples coming to mind as we talk. There will be many illustrations of his thoughtfulness when, even in suffering and pain, he had remembered the one who was caring for him, and had made some suggestion or foregone some attention that the burden of the one who was caring for him might be lightened. Maybe we learned later that he had suffered in silence rather than make a request that would have relieved him but would have placed an added demand upon his beloved.

The expression of appreciation will be an extended occupation. If the death breaks up a long marriage, the bereaved will have many memories of the years together that will call for such expression. Many incidents will have a meaning that they did not have at the time of their occurrence. Thoughtfulness, courage, and other positive traits which did not stand out at the time may come to mind with a new force. These memories will eventually go back and cover all the relationship together from the earliest beginning until the end.

With appreciation, and as a part of it, will go a certain amount of idealization. In addition to appreciating the positive values in the personality of the deceased there will be a viewing of him through rose-colored glasses. This may be especially true where the faults of the beloved threatened to overshadow his virtues. It is likely to be true in any case. These idealizations need to be expressed too. They need to be talked about unashamedly, and without hesitation.

Another type of idealization is to be expected from the mother who loses a small child or a baby. The loss will be not only what the deceased has been to the mother, but also a blow to her dreams of what the child might have become. Mourning over the loss of a newborn son may be filled with the mother's dreams of having him with her all the way from babyhood to manhood. It is only to be expected that this will be an idealized picture. The emotional reaction will be as real, however, as if the child had actually lived, and the need for talking about these pictures is as urgent as the need for talking about the memories of one whom she had known for a long time.

If anger or hostility is present, that needs to be talked about too. Feelings of anger or hostility may mingle with feelings of appreciation or may alternate with them. They should be talked about as they come. We are human and so was our beloved. It is inevitable that there should have been times of conflict or at least resentment or disappointment. If we feel the need to talk about these now, we should by all means do so. If other bereaved persons are wholly honest with themselves and with us, most of them will admit having similar feelings to a greater or lesser degree, and mostly of greater. Even if our hostile feelings are stronger in a particular bereavement situation than someone's else seemed to be in another situation, that does not mean any failure on our part. Practically it means only one thing, namely, that we have a greater need to talk about our hostile feelings than the other person did.

If there were times when the beloved seemed thoughtful, there may have been other times when he seemed inconsiderate and demanding. There may have been times when we felt that we needed rest more than the one now departed needed attention, yet attention was demanded, and our rest and sleep were broken up. The ill person for whom we were caring may have been fearful of being left alone nights, so that, even though little actual care was needed, we were unnecessarily robbed of our rest to cater to his apprehensions. Again, even though the demands of the ill were not unreasonable, and our affection was strong, there may reasonably have arisen certain questions as to whether we should be required to limit all our time and energies to caring for one who, perhaps, has had his or her life, while ours is slipping away without an opportunity for the full realization of our ambitions and talents.

Many variations of occasions for hostile feelings exist, too, where no lingering illness has been involved. Long companionship in marriage makes for appreciation, but it also makes for a full realization of the partner's weaknesses and failings. These may have been accepted and allowed for during life, but a discussion of them may well enter into the appraisal of the deceased. A feeling of the husband's inadequacy as a provider may be very irritating indeed, and the irritation may come out more fully into the open after his death. A wife may have been something of a baby in complaints about the heavy burden that care for the children put upon her, or she may have seemed to have an insatiable need for money beyond her husband's ability to provide or to understand the need for the expenditures. A child, though young and "innocent," may nevertheless have been a real source of irritation. Whatever the incident or occasion for the hostility or anger, the need for expression through talking out these feelings is the same. To dissolve our grief we must deal with anger and hostility as well as with sorrow and appreciation.

Instead of being directed at the deceased, hostility may be directed at some other person actually or presumably involved with our loved one's death. The attending physician is a favorite target. He may have delayed his coming when he was called. He may not have realized the seriousness of our loved one's illness soon enough. He should have sent our loved one to the hospital sooner, or maybe he shouldn't have sent him at all. It is easy in the time of loss to feel that if only the right thing had been done at the right time, the death might not have occurred. Maybe it isn't the physician. Maybe there is some member of the family who didn't show proper consideration, or even abused the one now deceased. Again, the possibilities of objects for our hostility are numerous, but the crux of the matter is the need that we have to talk out the feelings that beset us.

With sorrow, appreciation, and hostility go also guilt feelings which have an urgent need for release through talking. These feelings may be comparatively weak or strong. They may be directed to some specific incident, or they may be vague and generalized. They may be real or they may be fancied. Whatever their character, they still need to be dealt with by being consciously faced and resolutely brought out into the open. To be sure, this is not always the way of our strongest inclination. Often, when we have done something that we feel we ought not to have done, our tendency is to hide the fact from others if we can. Our own psychological needs demand, however, that we do talk out our guilt feelings as well as other emotional tensions. It is too late to do for the deceased the things that should have been done in his lifetime, but not too late for us to find health in confession and forgiveness.

After having courageously faced our loss, lived through our memories, and talked out our tensions, the next step is to renew old relationships with other people, or to form new ones. No one individual will fill the gap left by the beloved who has died. Neither will any group of individuals. That one was a special person who occupied a unique and deep place all his own in our life. Nevertheless a number of more casual friendships can help to fill the empty space. As social beings, we need the support of friendships and the occupation of social intercourse. Friends won't take the place of the deceased, but they will help us to bear our loss.